Pilgrim Poet ~ Roaming Rebel

Other Books
by Eric G. Müller

Novels:
Rites of Rock
Meet Me at the Met

Children's Book:
The Invisible Boat

Short Stories:
Drops on the Water
(Strories of Growing Up from a Father and Son)
(Coauthor: Matthew Zanoni Müller)

Poetry:
Coffee on the Piano for You
Frogs, Frags & Kisses
Life Poems for My Students

To fellow pilgrims, poets, roamers and rebels

Pilgrim Poet
Roaming Rebel

Eric G. Müller

Alkion Press

ISBN -10: 0-692-60293-3
ISBN-13: 978-0-692-60293-5

First Edition

Printed in the USA

Published in 2016
by Alkion Press
14 Old Wagon Road
Ghent, NY 12075

Title: Pilgrim Poet ~ Roaming Rebel
Author: Eric G. Müller
Cover: and interior photos: Eric G. Müller
Author Photo: Martina Angela Müller

Contents

Part One
Pilgrim Poet

Part Two
Roaming Rebel

Foreword

One of the most common and pernicious of human experiences is the feeling of knowing that you have had an idea, some fleeting insight perhaps, but you no longer know what it was. A special moment missed. Add a few thousand of these together and we have what Coleridge calls "the lethargy of custom." We lose hold on life if we confuse the familiar with the ordinary like this. For the reality is that we are continually surrounded by the extraordinary, though the lethargy of custom will blind us to this great fact, if we let it.

An active imagination living in wakeful senses is the only way of overcoming this. Thank goodness, then, for poets like Eric G. Müller who show us how it's done. You are holding in your hand a book, which is a product of just this discipline of imaginatively grasping the fleeting moment. And it is also a demonstration of the equally great fact that any one of these moments is an entry point into the depths and heights of the human spirit. Müller never stints his attention – it is given with equal devotion to pebbles and to great works of art, and with equally tangential effects. In these poems the occasional meets the perpetual in an exhilarating dance that expresses love of life, the quirky individuality of perception and the close kinship between the pilgrim and the rebel.

~ Norman Skillen

Introduction

My urge to wander the world has drawn me to sundry historic and holy sites, where I can feel their ethos, and sense the gossamer pull of deeds done, thoughts felt, lives lived. Within those hallowed, or occasionally hellish locales – depending where my steps have taken me – I find my words loosening, letting me carve and curve them onto paper, nudged by an imperceptible hand. And, in turn, my tongue is moved to sound the re-formed thoughts back into the ether, the font from whence they came – transformed to make some difference, no matter how slight. And as such the polarities of my auxiliary self merge: the rebel pilgrim and roaming poet.

The pull of ancient and sacred sites is an ongoing pattern that keeps on repeating itself throughout my life. It's as if I can only find the right relation to the future by seeking out consecrated destinations from the past. There's a mystique that lives in these sacred places that I can latch onto as soon as I take the time to listen, empty and open. Running parallel to these sites are the elusive and grand works of nature in their manifold manifestations to which I cannot help but pay reverent homage.

Museums too are a kind of sanctified preserve that broaden the mind and soften the soul in gratitude for what the human spirit has achieved throughout the ages, from the distant past to the present day. And I never know what, if anything, will tug at my heightened perceptions, or knock on my senses' doors. I often find myself in a state of blank suspension, till something activates the inner fisherman, and I can reel in the creative catch of an ekphrastic poem or a new insight.

And lastly, it's the people I meet and seek out along the way, who enrich the moments through their uniqueness. Each meeting is a gift, the significance of which I might never fully comprehend. And in each of these festooned sojourns I let the germinating process take its course.

I've often stood apart, due to circumstance and my nature. Moving from place to place throughout my childhood started the pattern that I've continued to thread to this day: from town to town, country to country, from one continent to another. I became an observer, and though I always endeavored to fit in, something was always amiss, off, or foreign.

As a budding adolescent my outsider status embodied itself in the rebel. I noted injustices at every turn: from dire poverty and the discriminating Apartheid system in South Africa, to the antiquated educational methods that I was subject to and forced to succumb. I spoke up, took action. Armed with pen and paper I became a literary sniper, shooting bullet words from the safety of my hidden retreats. The shots went wide and unheard, but they served as target practice for future word volleys. Simultaneously, I was on a quest for deeper meaning and transcendent truths, to nurture and nourish my spiritual hunger. These secular and sacred motivators have accompanied me ever since, forming a fluid lemniscate through which I move effortlessly, the rebel and the pilgrim, the one always connected to the other.

Many of the poems in this collection were penned during the more recent trips my wife and I undertook to Italy, Turkey and Greece, though some were written in Switzerland, Germany, Greece, England, Costa Rica and, of course, while traveling through America.

And a small batch was composed right here at home — private paeans to peace, or covert declarations of war against some inequality, dissatisfaction or discontent. Still, in one way or another, I owe these poems to the achievements of countless freethinkers, visionaries, leaders, artists and nonconformists across the ages — in short, fellow rebels and pilgrims!

~ Eric G. Müller

Part One

Pilgrim Poet

Winds of Ilium

The wind brought
wealth to Troia

The taxi brought us
to that walled citadel
after an aborted wait
for a no-show otobüs
that left me mad
like *Iliad's* wrath ridden Achilles

The wind brought
wealth to Troia

My decades old dream
drove me to the nine circles
of pre and post Hellas ruins
where the hillock breeze
whispers unearthed tales through
the leafy fig tree under which I sit

The wind brought
wealth to Troia

Now its fleets of luxury buses
beached in the parking lot
packed with fast-touch tourists
rich in devices of every ilk
for an hour's quick fix –
ready to be checked off the culture list

The wind brought
wealth to Troia

And as my Achaean anger subsides
wind-waves comb gradual calm
through my hair and heart
coaxing me to listen
and latch onto prime treasures –
winged and free for the taking

The wind still brings
wealth to Troia

~ Written under a fig tree next to the Schliemann
Trench

Polymastic Goddess

Hardly anybody bothers
to come here much
and the few who do
step off the bus for seconds
then quickly retreat
to the tinted interior
of AC cooled comfort
or get chased away
by hissing geese
that guard the grounds'
grassy threshold
of toppled pillars and
abandoned boulders
with gendarme authority

Hard to think
this morass of a place
midst nature's budding sprawl
topped the mythic list
of the ancient world's
Seven Wonders
where only one solitary column
crowned with a scrappy nest
of sentinel storks now remains
to remind us of Artemisia's temple
the Polymastic Goddess
(sometimes said to be laced with bulls' scrotal sacs)
who housed in its hallowed hidden cella

Swallows swirl
and dive for insects
above the swamp
where turtles, frogs and water snakes
keep something alive

of the mysteries
that glow in the slow
revolving zodiac
behind nature's wrap
which the hierophants
of Leto's lush daughter –
Apollo's chaste sister
knew how to loosen and unravel
but now are lost

Ruins of the Temple of Artemis ~ Ephesus, Turkey

Artemis

Ayasuluk Summit

Where else
but on this
hill of love
can I find
kernels of
the Word?

The place
where the aged
Theologian chose
to sit and pray
and write
the Logos script

What else
but to wait
till I'm good
and ready
to grow
a word more wise

~ After paying homage to Saint John the Evangelist at his tomb within the ruins of the Basilica of Saint John, I gradually made my way up to the top of Ayasuluk Hill, stepping through the massive walls of the remains of the Grand Fortress that surrounds the hilltop. It is said that

the venerable prophet wrote his Gospel on top of that very hill. I found myself alone, and imagined the ancient apostle in that hallowed place, praying, writing, and sunk in deep contemplation. After inhaling the view I sat on a rock and receded into a meditative mode, accompanied by a gentle breeze and a fly or two, after which I penned the poem.

Eagle's End

Circling down to earth
the Eagle lands in a hole
up on a wide hill.
With sunk head he folds his wings
and waits for the storm to come.

Water fills the grave;
loose earth caves in and buries
the feathery oval –
freed, he pierces through the rage
and spreads his cry to the stars.

Next day in the sun
surrounding the wet-mud tomb
many have gathered –
flocks of different feathers
with folded wings, remembering.

At the dawn of dusk
the hill rises up as one
old songs sung anew to the
world

Selcuk, Turkey

Athena Temple

Athena, in keeping with her
High birth from Zeus' sky head
On thin-air Olympus

Has her temples planted
From acropolis to acropolis
Securing owl-eyed views above seas

Mountains and men
From where fierce eyed Pallas
Can encourage the young

To find their independence
And the strong to reach
Their rebel goals

To the relief of the weak and wronged
While lending her thought spear
To the many she minds and mentors

Together with an olive branch –
Both gifts of nighttime knowledge
As Guides to the day

~ Written just below the Athena Temple in the welcome shade of a canopied Stone Pine at the ancient Kamiros Ruins in Rhodes, Greece

Elementals

With a mere gaze
I free the Invisibles –
the sandillions
sacrificially caught
so that we may strut
the terra firma

Maybe not so mere –
for my senses' probes
are flushed with
well practiced care
for the hidden enclaves
that crave to be sought

So that the Invisibles –
trapped between
the material codes
can be revealed
by our mere
Attention

*~ Anfandou, after an outing to Petaloudes-Butterfly
Valley in Rhodes, Greece*

And Still the Birds Tumble

Clouds bleed bullet
birds
above starved lamb
sleeping
between angels-turn-
human
while bats rip open their
chests
dropping hot tar
dreams
over winged skull with woman's
smirk
into knuckle-sockets onto spiral
knees
below cracked cranium
listening
to jawbone-arms
prattle
twisted lies that
lie
around the bone-mount as the
hand
of the lowered shroud-body
rests
in a veiled lap like a
fish
with one blood-eye
reading
her unlocked barefoot
book

near a cross-drill that blinds the
disc-I-ple
and still the birds
tumble
when lotus flower-flames
open
around the nailed lamb that
offered
His last breath as the
tomb
shuddered and the ashes
flickered

Never Just Nothing

It's never just nothing –
dust was and will be

something other –

Spores and seeds lead to more –
even a vacuum is an

in between

a womb waiting for a
flash in the curving

firm-amen-t when

ousted semen stars fight
to survive the Big current of the

silent Bang

and plosive aftershocks
ripple down into

measured matter

Shaped by time's space
and the crises we know are

never just nothing

~ *'And Still the Birds Tumble' and 'Never Just Nothing' I wrote after viewing an exhibition of Albrecht Dürer's woodcuts at the Clark Museum, Williamstown, MA*

Folded Arms

His arms weren't always folded,
But hung to his side
Till the pain in his heart
Grew too strong and He
Lifted them to the wound,
Folding the world in his embrace,
Like protective wings,
Warming the hurt into
One love that shone through
His red robe and wrist,
Where it lingered for a while
Like a little sun.

Now, his face a little pale, and
Tilted slightly to his right,
Patiently ponders what must come;
And for a moment his hair
Hardens into a crown
Of thorns that he'll
Soon be wearing, bearing,
Till his skin bleeds
Dew dabbed roses.

Glens Falls in upstate New York is an unlikely place to come across a Rembrandt van Rijn painting. 'Christ with Folded Arms' is part of the Hyde Collection, one of many treasures in that small but fine art museum. X-rays show that the arms were originally down at his side, a fact that intrigued and inspired me to write the poem.

Calyx

there's a growing
Grail
that catches the
Light
and makes things
Grow –
it holds the
World
in its cupped
Hands
like a protective
Calyx
from which the petals
Spread

up close this
Chalice
is made from
Millions
of tiny flower
Cups
which is the
Result
of our own
Slow
growth to become
Crucibles
for catching and giving
Light

After leaving the Basilica of Francesco d'Assisi, I went walking through the medieval town of Assisi, slowly winding my way up through the narrow cobblestoned alleys, stopping now and again to look over the expansive Umbrian landscape. It felt good to walk after sitting in the darkened crypt by the tomb of Saint Francis, where I'd let the frescos by Giotto and Cimabue from the lower and upper churches settle. As I made my way up the slopes of the hill of Asio, away from the crowds, the word 'calyx' entered my mind, and the poem unfurled.

Space Made

Using thought fabric
made from mind's dew
I fashion a dome
to keep out the noise
and create a space
in which Silence
can

breathe

Dropping grains
that grow into mood
swaying the atmosphere
in which judgment
remains withheld
until the New
enters the space

made

Private Prayer

Round the corner of the
Basilica Di San Lorenzo's
Main portal, a sign reads:
Free entrance for private prayer.

So I find a pew
   and fake a prayer;
Close my eyes
   and fold my hands,
And clear my mind to
   write a poem.

No words come,
   but when I leave
I feel as free
   as if I'd entered into
Private prayer.

~ Florence, Italy

Between Hands

What really happens in
between the hands of one
person and another?

This I wonder as I
ponder the space
between the Angel

and Mary in Botticelli's
"Cestello Annunciation"
where the holy "Yes"

and innocent "No"
of their tender hands
form a promise

of something more
that still is less
than nothing.

And I think back
to God and Adam
taking center-ceiling

in the Sistine Chapel –
their hands reaching
for one another –

fingers almost touching…

Or your own two hands
when they fold
curve and clasp

as they work together...

Hands, the limbs
that give form to the
movements of the heart.

~ Uffizi Gallery, Florence, Italy

Stole

In the vestibule of the basilica
she stole a blue veil
and aired it gently
over her black-haired head

She smiled as she felt
the cloth flow down to her knees
bending to the movement till the stone
in its cool embrace welcomed her

Folded low she sprinkled
her blessings over the marble slabs
that softened and gave way
to the earth beneath

The earth drank her
Heart – while she hid
her shame beneath
her new-won stole

*~ Written in St. Peter's Church – April 29, 2011 – day
before Pope JP II's beatification*

Pietà

What arcane prescience
made one-eared Vincent
paint the Pietà during the
raven-year of his own
premature death?

There,
no longer bent over the native soil
the peasant Madonna leans forward
in her churning, wild, blue garment,
giving Him away,

like a fruit of the field,
those she's harvested, tended
and handed out her whole life long.

And in her sacrifice she offers
the worn and battered body
to the world,
while her smile holds the knowledge
she's gained from nature
that all death is seed to new life –
never more than now!

What holy premonition
made this priestly painter
depict himself in the limp likeness
of the one who is hated
more than he is loved?

His death,
the sleep
from which
we have to awake –
A wake.

Poems surprise. I never know when and where a poem might draw near, urging for embodiment. And oftentimes they make themselves felt in unlikely places. I've learned to be prepared. While strolling through the Vatican in Rome I assumed that my penchant for writing would be stimulated by Renaissance paintings, Roman sculptures or the frescoes in the Stanze di Raffaello. However, it was Vincent Van Gogh's rendering of the Pietà that stirred my creative juices. The painting is easily missed, as it is located in a tiny gallery in the contemporary sacred art section. I sat alone and at peace in the conveniently situated bay window, contemplating the small painting without any interruption, while most people hurried by to see the Sistine Chapel.

Tower and Steeple

Swallows swoop and whistle
between tower and steeple

binding the sacred and the secular
with their exhilarating chase

making light of the perennial
war of opposites

that smacks us
to our senses

*~ Florence, Italy, while looking out the window of the
Casa Santo Nome di Gesu*

Transfiguration

The hands   as eyes
and eyes   as marks
of perception

that sense   to see
how the transfigured   One
can transfigure

the many   who are
plagued or terror stricken
by this or that.

Stern faced   Faith
kneels her modest
bare-beauty-body

and points to the   boy
possessed by squint-vision –
her bold eyes declaring

This too is you

as the Apostles'   helpless
eyes and hands are   moved
in their own wordless   way.

The crowd is still   severed
from the full   force
of the softened   sun

and the light is still too   severe
for the fallen disciples
on Tabor Hill

shying away and shielding themselves
from the lifting   cloud
of the flame-blue   logos.

Cool pre-figuration of the
ascending Gardener in his
death defying   body

who awaits to succumb
to the dreadful   deed
that will shake

the other   hill –
the rock-fist of   skulls
and triple   death.

Only what divides is   dark
and that too
can be   climbed

with foot and handholds
to help us   feel
our   way   up.

~ Sitting in the Pinacoteca Vaticana, contemplating Raphael's 'Transfiguration,' his last painting, his favorite

Question

What does it mean
when daily thousands pass by the
Raffaello Sanzio da Urbino tomb
in La Cupola Del Pantheon

paying homage
to the man who painted
The School of Athens
and other illimitable masterpieces

       in front
       of which
       thousands more
       pass by
         ?

~ In the Pantheon, Rome

This Tree

This tree grew from the ground up
with just two branches
jutting out near the top
to the left and to the right

This tree was all black
with 12 white doves
that landed and graced
the trunk and limbs

And on this tree was nailed a man
who didn't seem to mind too much
bearing it with a merciful shrug
knowing it had to come to pass

This tree grew from a bush of green
under which a rabbit nibbled
and two deer that tugged
and bit down to the roots

This tree was an anchor
dropped into the earth
by the Captain himself
who wanted his crew to find firm footing

This tree is in the garden
which we need to tend
along with all the others
who walk along its
groves and flower beds

This tree will fall
and when it does
the doves will fly away
and perch in the palm
that offers seeds to peck

This tree is you and me
the bond we share and bear

~ Contemplating the mosaic in the Basilica of San Clemente, Rome, Italy

Pilgrim's Palm

In the valley between
thumb and pointer
a village nestles
where pilgrims gather
to process down the lifeline
to the junction where fate
determines the brambly path
and young dame Destiny
weeps...

filling the well for the weary
knowing of the maze ahead
that's crisscrossed with choices
the easiest of which lead toward
Fingers' End where sharp
nails scratch a coded map
deep into the flesh
leaving scars they need to read
in order to get back
home

~ Monterosso, Cinque Terre, Italy

The Last Judgment

No escape for the naked hoard
blasted into the abyss
with fanfare trumpets
by angelic cherubs
perched on firm-thin clouds
stripping the sinners of any
hope

Horned hogs and wild horses
trample the freshly fallen flesh-grapes
underneath their horn-sickle hoofs
leaving the pulp to ferment
into blood-wine for
Belzebub's frenzied
helpers

Some sit stunned
in their disemboweled state
their gray spines exposed
as the sinewy demon-lackeys
move on to the next
with their primitive tools of
torture

Between the twisted bodies
a 7 headed serpent
bares its cumulative fangs
ready to down 7 miscreants
with one hiss of a stroke
escorted by flying snake-swans
to take care of the dodging rest

Desperate women sink their teeth
into one another like rabid apes
while a bald, randy Bachus
hops on a straggler and smashes
his gob with a grapefruit-rock
in front of a spent
four-boobed wench

A looming and three-faced
monster-man with spiral antlers
and massive-membrane wings
spread wide like a peacock erection
casually devours a nude
and kicking Adonis
headfirst

To his left a muscled ogre
shoves a long, sturdy rod
with a flaming mop-head
up the anus of a contorted reprobate
while a hefty nearby sister
has a fire-fisted pole
twisted deep into her vagina-eye

And the stripped bodies
keep on tumbling
into the wail-pit of
broken, dismembered humanity
driving the demons and fellow deviants
crazy in their lust to mete out
pain and misery

Only scythe-armed Death
and old man Time – who extends
the you-got-it-coming hourglass –
stand tall and still in the inferno
that's painted in the cupola
for the frail congregants to apprehend
while caught up in fear inducing rhetoric

All this in Firenze's Duomo
where the Last Judgment
should invoke
compassion –
    Not
the revenge-lust
of Roman law

~ While climbing to the top of the Cattedrale di Santa Maria del Fiore in Florence, Italy, better known as the Duomo, I stopped on the landing underneath the huge dome to study Vasari's painting of the 'Last Judgment' in the cupola. My disquieting disturbances are stitched into the poem.

He Let it Happen

He let it happen,
  the kiss, the spitting;
He let it happen,
  the mocking and cursing;
He let it happen,
  the whipping and beating;
He let it happen,
  the ongoing goading to Golgotha
He let it happen,
  the nailing, the pounding;
He let it happen,
  the crowning and crucifixion;
He let it happen,
  the final thrust of Longinus' lance
He let it happen,
  knowing
It had to happen;
It all had to happen,
  except for the breaking
  of his bones;
That could Not happen
  so that the rest
  Could Happen.

~ Written after viewing the frescoes by Fra Angelico in San Marco, Florence, Italy

A Part in Us

there is a part in us
that betrays

it's the yeast
that makes us rise

it's the beast
that makes us fall

we get baked
or burned

depending on whether we
remember or forget

the part in us
that betrays

~ *San Marco, Florence, Italy*

In the Way

We're often in the way
of one another –
blocking the flow
like rocks in a river

Often we're in the way
of ourselves –
caught in the current
smashing rocks in a flood

The way to the other
is often through
the flow of minds –
across stepping stones…

To make way
for others
and ourselves
is to be a rock
or a river
depending on
the need
of the moment

~ San Marco, Florence, Italy

Vessels

goblets, glasses,
pewters, pitchers,
jars, jugs,
cups, cauldrons,
mugs, magnums,
bottle, basins,
vials, vases;

filled and emptied,
emptied and filled,
broken, mended, discarded –
and found;
round and around
and upside down
and maybe back upright;

their form
mostly veiled
through function,
like you from me –
mostly
us from them –
mostly.

~ Vatican Museum, inspired by a still life by Giorgio Morandi

Part Two

Roaming Rebel

Allen Ginsberg in Atlantis

Await you hero-head of the Beat-butt age ...
chair still empty, table covered in saffron silk,
chimes, cymbals and red-box-incense, dancing
Shiva, books, piled papers – circled by the low
throat-hum of Moloch's sentinels –

Black devouring boxes to amplify your howl
against the mind which made them master.
Heard you, American mantra man, feet lifting,
shifting, to the tidal drifting of your pulsing heart;

Pounding, pouncing, down, up and around;
holy spray spewing from your fleshy lips.
And what you stood for you still are:
a Blakian hobo-homo-mystic-man – ah, men! –

How you mad-milked the mythic harmonium,
plastered with memento stickers from Dylan's
Rolling Thunder Revue Tour, getting the jiving
mob to chant along to the lamb-soft strain of

    ... all the hills echoed
   And all the hills echoed
   And all the hills echoed
   And all the hills echoed
   And all the hills echoed
   And all the hills ...

*~ Atlantis Club ~ December 5, 1980, three days before
John Lennon got shot*

Thinking about Emily

She died where she lived
in her upstairs 'Paradise'
of light and words
pacing from window to corner window

On occasion she took
a thinly coiled cord and let
her wit descend – on the taste
of sweet smelling gingerbreads

to the gleam-eyed delight
of the cheerful gathering of
jumping children – before quickly
reeling in the frail umbilical rope

that still kept her loosely linked
to the life she once had led

~ *Written after visiting the Emily Dickinson House in Amherst, Massachusetts – up the road, over cappuccino, in the Black Sheep Café*

Honey Hag

The wizened Cretan widow
dressed in well-worn black
smiled with patterned wrinkles
which coiled all the way back
to the Minoan Snake Goddess

She broke off two chunks
of flat braided bread – warm –
insisting we taste the sweetness
right there and then

and as we chewed
with our nodding jaws
we sank into
a sleepy zone
of milk and honey

giving new meaning
to the term – breaking bread

Rendered helpless we bought
the embroidered tablecloth
as the honey-hag chuckled
sending her tongued wrinkles
slithering down to her hands

as she tucked away the money

~ *Crete, Greece*

Mahatma Malala

Mahatma Malala
what details of the day did you discuss
as you stepped on the bus
surrounded by the chirp & giggle of
other girls?

Mahatma Malala
what must you have thought when a masked man
who roared up on a motorbike, drew the green
drape aside and stuck his head into the back of the
dusty van?

Mahatma Malala
what fear, if any, did you feel when the hooded
militant pointed his pistol through the shredded
shrieks of schoolgirls shouting – which one of you
is Malala?

Mahatma Malala
what courage must blaze in you
having known all along they'd hunt you down
and punish you for exposing
their evil?

Mahatma Malala
what ineffable drive moved you to resist and speak
out against the will and mayhem of the Taliban –
the burning of schools to sever
girls' education?

Mahatma Malala
you could not have heard the twin shots
that hit you in the head & neck
and wounded two more chaste-veiled
daughters

Mahatma Malala
you must know that your mellow voice for peace
is louder than any shots fired to spread fear
instead of freedom in the Swat Valley
of the world

Mahatma Malala
you are the future of a force
grander and greater than all blind
fanaticism that tries to impose its
cowardly will

Mahatma Malala
you sum up tomorrow's women
a feminine force that leads to light
the threatened masculine rage
through love

Mahatma Malala
you, a mere 14 year old
have shown what each of us
can do to change life for the
better

Mahatma Malala
may you survive the wounds you took
for all who suffer undue bondage
for spreading – not Western – but
human thinking

Mahatma Malala
Great Soul Malala
your voice –
it lives
on

~ *When I heard the news, on October 9, 2012 that Malala Yousafzia was shot by the Taliban I was shocked like thousands of others. As I went to bed that night the words "Mahatma Malala" swiveled round my mind like an endless mantra. The next morning I wrote this poem.*

I Heard

I heard a butterfly
Dragging a chain
I heard it cry
Down the lane
I heard a fly
Hammering nails
I heard a lullaby
Between two rails

~ *Forest Row, England*

Election

At the eleventh hour,
Seconds after the lapidary announcement
By the late night anchorman was made,
I was shoved down onto the piano stool
And told to play, while the crowd whooped
And chanted, "Play, play, play!"

My mind went stone blank and
The moment stretched into a mile
While my fingers stroked the Ivory Coast,
Overpowered by the music I was supposed
To make to underscore the monumental event,
Pushed by a crowd high with hope.

My fingers took over and sailed across the black
And white keys, with a slow, slow blues that
Launched a hundred thousand slavers into the
Salt-soaked desert, while my right hand witnessed
their tortured passage across,

And my left hand's relentless beat
Saw them sold and separated,
In a rampage of wails and
Cries, calls and hollers,
Shouts and
Shrieks.

I played on through the centuries, paying homage
To all the hurt ever uttered by the abused minority
Under the pale yoke of savage discrimination –
Till quite warmed up I broke the chains of bondage
To the chant of, "Yes we can," – and shifted to a
Major key.

~ Pondering Obama's historic election of 11/04/08

William's Secret

Over tea you once told me
That your name has
Will and *I am* in it

I laughed and said
Mine has *mule* and *err*

But his words fit perfectly
While mine do not.

And you told me further
How much *will* it takes
To fully realize one's *I am*.

And how your name
Was a daily reminder
Of the developing self.

It is the credo
By which you live;

It lives in every chuckle
And word you speak

But the secret of your name
Holds more in store
Than even you can know

For any time we intone
Your name, we are divining
A secret message of becoming

And because you have practiced it
Your will spreads into us

By calling out your name, "William,"
We strengthen our resolve to be

In your relentless pursuit of the *I am*
You've looked the logos in the eye
And become the ward of the word

~ In loving memory of William Ward – teacher, writer, preacher, rebel, jokester, sage

Garden Deal

Never let the palmed shuffle go too wild while
flipping through yellowed notepads where
abandoned gardens let hosepipe philosophy
grow amongst tall weeds that trip the nether-
mind's best intentions.

It only releases the pierce-eyed detective who
tours the lasting cliffs of tacked mugshots
across shiny walls and florescent fatigue
as he joins clues with fat black sharpies

Spreading the insects' dissected sentences
throughout the precinct's inner sanctum
where the manhunt takes on ritual significance,
until a choreographed dance along the contours of
symbolic scrawls breaks through the muck

Too often we're fooled to think we've found
the rare fruit, fantasizing how the squeezed juice
flits across our animal tongues, in everlasting
hope-drops that whet our desire for more

But burns across the perennial red carpet
igniting the papillae into crumbling pillars
crushed to sand in night's frozen pockets
to sift through time's ticking fingers

As we reminisce how sweet
the other's flesh tasted
when the buds still stood supple and guilt free
while we thrilled your way out of Eden

Starved and always aching for the fruit we stole
forgetting that freedom's crop lies in the
spit-in-the-palm deal between hunter and hunted
to go at it together – to tend that garden for all

~ While driving along the Taconic State Parkway to Chatham, NY, the words of the poem percolated through the purr of the engine, warming the wet surface of my tarmac mind.

Storks

Two storks bend
back their thin
curved necks
and clapper with red

abandon, before
copulating in a flutter of black
and white on top
of Mount Ayatoulouk's

highest column

overlooking Saint John's quiet
tomb, resting in the ruins
of the greatest church
of the ancient East.

Moments later they soar
into the evening blue
and circle in the afterglow
of their thrill.

~ Selcuk, Turkey at the ruins of St. John's Cathedral

Muddy Water Dance

On the bus from Cinque Terre,
on the western coast of Italy
we pass a river that's drying
with thousands of fish

stranded in the shallows, dying;
making the muddied waters dance,
as they frantically jump and shiver
under the hot Ligurian sun,

with fat, languid gulls
squatted all along this
frenzied bed of impending death,
picking them out one by one.

We drive on to Florence,

leaving this rush of life behind,
and I picture how this trembling tongue,
spluttering with spirit,
will soon be silent and bare.

~ *Between La Spezia and Florence, Italy*

Sitka Spruce

Once my hand
Lay flat against
The giant Sitka Spruce

I felt its age and might
Ring through from
The distant center.

Its firm bark,
Furry with moss,
flung messages

From its crown-top antenna –
Signals I could not decode,
But kept on listening for.

No touch of any hide or pelt
From the wildest bear or bison bull
Could make me tingle more.

But as I continued,
Holding hand to massive trunk,
I sensed the muscles of this

Wooden mastodon
Begin to stir –
Shaking my tiny hand…

And now, much later,
I still feel the warmth
Of his latent squeeze.

So What!

So what
If you don't know
this or that!

As long as you still listen to the wind
hush through trees, or lash across
mountains, deserts or dunes;

and with closed eyes can detect the subtle shifts
in the nasals, plosives and fricatives of nature's
complex tongue as it tells its simple tales.

So what
if you don't know
this or that!

As long as you keep the lenses
of all your senses clean – so you can make sense
of a world, made senseless by indoor knowledge.

What if you knew
the real from the false?
What if?

Now that would be
the kind of knowledge
that would make sense!

~ *The two preceding poems were written on the Oregon
Coast at Cape Perpetua, near Yachats*

Boats

Bouquet
of boats
anchored
in the rocky harbor
taking
a snooze
by the calyx
of cafes –
their dolphin smile hulls
pointing
like petal arrows
into the
waiting
ocean

~ Lindos, Rhodes, Greece

Pebbles

In my writing
I always have to
make do
with pebbles
on the floor
instead
of marble sculptures
in the sky

~ *Archeological Museum in Rhodes, Greece, sipping a frappe*

Catchers

Hearts dangle in the wind –
    Dream Catchers
But left hanging
Over empty chairs

Open urns commiserate –
    Rain Catchers
but left tilted
by a pool of ash

Palm fronds fan out –
    Sun Catchers
but left dry
in a bed of sand

Sun rains on dreams –
    Life Catchers
But left for us
To see and tend

~ *Afandou Beach, Rhodes, Greece at Al Mare Café*

Coffee Date

A 4 footed shoe-sigh
On Banjo Café welcome mat
tugs at 2 cups, brown,
waiting to fill with
the thrill-screech
of fine foam, white;

shot with double
espresso, black,
to secrete change.

Soon thoughts link arms
and tongue-tips touch,
waltzing around in
uni-chamber, pink,
while the future
stirs in secret.

~ *Banjo Mountain Café, Harlemville NY*

Seven Sips of Coffee

A toy dog in a basket fixed on a bicycle
speeds by with his geriatric master

Still as a sculpture on the concrete floor
a green iguana with mandala skin listens

Four tanned surfers swagger along
With decorative boards and butt-crack shorts

Bikini babes with curling tattoos
laugh to the rhythm of their flip-flops

Bored security guard plugged to an iPod
Taps his baton as he walks his beat

Two plain blue nuns with homemade habits
Look hot, i.e. sweaty and out of place

A boy pops wheelies
With his bike on the pavement

This is what I spied in the seven sips
It took me to quaff my cappuccino

~ *Jaco, Costa Rica*

In the Café

In the café
I get to say "Hello,"
to faces from
here and there;
each one
conjuring memories
that keep changing,
making me wonder
whether I was
a gift or a burden;
because we can
always grow,
letting the meeting fade
into another memory
to add substance
to the next "Hello"
in the Café

~ Chatham, NY

Diner Ennui

two men in a diner climb
over chairs and wink
at the waitress who laughs as she flips
a burger and rumbles through
a gallery of refined curses

overwhelming the pot bellied grump
in slot 24 who never tips
but fancies himself a Don
holding forth to his gang
of water-eyed veterans

two nubile girls sucking shakes
conduct noisy diary-logues and swoon
at future memories as they cough
and page through male torso mags
till nobody comes to the rescue

The barstool beggar who cannot choose
hears a violin that sings of
frost and Japanese blossoms
and wonders if he'll ever dare
to fix the holes the Beatles left untended

Lone man trying to thread a moment with his pen

~ At a Diner somewhere in New Hampshire

KO

Across the track
in the trailer park
lot 58
a voice-plagued pugilist
forgets his losses
slumped in the corner
of the stained settee
reeking of urine
near the TV
where he gropes with his fists
for one last bout
with the bottle
round eleven
sobbing when the sitcom
takes a sentimental turn
and the laughing tracks
fly into a roar
roping him in

His killer left
silences the crowd
with one deft jab
of the remote
and still he parries
through the channels
till he lets down his guard
to satisfy an unzipped itch
during a commercial break
leaving him shuddering
on the floor
as the night train
rings its warning bell

and sounds its
long-long-short-long whistle

thirty seconds
from the intersection
where tomorrow he'll wait
to jump

She Got

she got grit between
her legs and in her loins

she got the pluck of a sharp-
tuned, barbed-wire banjo

and her washed out, moonshine-voice
traps hope with a wistful sigh

she got the shunt and steam
of a locomotive's ache

she got tears to "salt the bacon"
and a cool-cool halo above it all

*"KO" and "She Got" were triggered by some vagrants I
spotted*

Depressed

The black case is
Closed.
The six strings don't
Vibrate,
Nor the others, the 3, 4 and
More.
And all those vinyl records lie
Untouched
In the basement next to the trap-set –
Dismantled.
Pipes, whistles and flutes remain
Unaired.
My room has turned into a
Mausoleum.
My peace is
Gone.
And I wait and pace for
Something –
Some thing to resurrect the
Dead.

~ *Spring equinox*

Sparklin' Water

Poured myself some sparkling
water – the bursting bubbles,
tiny drumbeats
against the crystal glass,
which rejoiced with a vibrant
      Yes in C#!
an invitation to jam along,
which I humbly did,
Sipping and humming around the
descending scale until I'd
downed the ambrosial draft
into silence,
though the sound still tingled on...

Dancing Sheaves

Dancing sheaves –
cone skirts flying wide
like whirling dervishes
in the wheat fields –
while the reaper
gives the rhythm
with his swinging
scythe

~ At the 'Van Gogh and Nature' exhibit at the Clark Museum, Williamstown – viewing "Wheat Stacks with Reaper"

At the Art Museum

Even though spiders
process through my nostrils
I dive into color aches
and pools of nostalgia

pulling me forward
as I fall back to linger
in memories that live
in drive-by-landscapes

whispering unintelligibly
while guards fiercely eye
the potential of destructive applause
taking cover from the cloudburst

that sends people running
to understand how to lengthen life
that's surrounded by
the thicket of time

*~ Written while perambulating through the Im-Ex
exhibition at the Old Museum, Berlin, Germany*

One Last

One last foray through the
Goodies swept to the side in a heap
As large as the Staten Island dump

One quick look to see
What's under the slab of stone
As heavy as the philosopher's sigh

One last nervous pluck
At thoughts that lead to creation's source
As elusive as yesterday's tomorrow

One last picnic on God's gated lawn
Trampled with the deep treads of
Disappointed hope and furrowed longing

One last appraisal of life in re-verse
To acknowledge that
It all depends on me – to see

~ Harlemville, NY

Ocean Climb

she climbed the ocean
and in the valley
she planted a cloud
attracting mourners
ululating praise
till she fell awake
releasing dreams
that hugged the walls
flipping the lids
letting puff-lings
lead her to the rim
of the toe-touched ocean
she'd climbed

~ Harlemville, NY

Arrow

My arrow is
blunt and not
very aerodynamic.
It's been handed
down through the generations,
used, abused and worn with age.

I am
the arrow's keeper –
it is my hunting tool.
I have to make do,
for it's the only one
I have.

But slowly, furtively
I fashion a new arrow:
Sharp and sleek,
made to hit the mark,
worthy of passing on
to emerging generations.

~ *Boboli Gardens, Italy*

Phantom Words

In the pre-sleep dark
words haunt me –
their hollow sounds
crowd my mind
like pebbles cracking
under the weight of the crush
or tickle my cheeks with
their tiny threads
that break each time I pull
or try to follow them
to their origin…
I'm left, severed from the source –
empty, crushed – laughing

~ Insomniac night, Ghent, NY

Tide

standing neck high
in the ocean
on the arc
of time –
rising tide

~ Afandou Beach, Rhodes, Greece

Thought Filaments

When the head clears
more dream-stencils are found
stuck in the watershed's denial

nowhere more obvious than in
the museum's hallways that run through
timeline-miles of the covert hunt

cutting across the stretched lifeline
scraped bloody by fate's barbed wire
then up the tangled heart-line – skipping

squandering opportunities
pouring gasoline over squashed
attempts of catching – holding on

flicking matches over drenched options
during the digestive pulse
wishing to square away the

rough curved bulge
between tightening urges
crawling with distractions

turning intentions into spectacles that
maneuver plans but refuse to
topple popping pleasures' chaos

though apologetic coughs are funneled
through retrospective lenses
as untamed horrors uncheck

veracity's buried beauty
elongated between the yin-yang twirl
and Om's egg shaped aperture

replenished in the switchback slide – educing
inhalations of alpine sparkle to hemorrhaged pity!
Saving the card-house-thoughts from destruction

Enthusiasm

Enthusiasm is an ephemeral thing –
trailing knowledge
from its hot wings
tickling others to spread their feathers
to take flight and follow thought
as it migrates
to places unimaginable

Enthusiasm is an ephemeral thing –
burning out while ashes
fall and find themselves
reformed and fixed in books
imparting cooled knowledge
between dead winged covers

Enthusiasm is an ephemeral thing –
fly with it and see
for however short
life from a higher
vantage point

Word Warts

words stuck
to his tongue
like warts

one by one
he crunched them
between his teeth

spitting, swallowing
and tearing off
the fleshy raisins

till the tongue
bloodied but freed
could again roll out

into a runway
or springboard
for words that matter

Whiplashed

whiplashed by echoes
pounding me with growing force
till I double up
under tolling decibels
that measures my undoing

~ Rhodes, Greece

Variations on YES

YES is more
and
NO is a door
that
opens
when you accept
the door that's
        shut

YES!
I do want –
But more than that
I want
Not to want!

Sometimes the NO
Is a necessary detour
To the YES

Sometimes the YES
Is an unnecessary way
Of saying NO

Both YES and NO
Depend on the context,
But in the end
YES is what we know
As love

The affirmative YES is a rare portal
If it stands on the firm foundation
Of a night-sealed NO

Roman Holiday

Golden King Tut freezes
for a few coins
next to a busking band
that plays an endless version of
"Autumn Leaves," while
Gladiators pose for photos and
flirt with the girls
to fatten their wallets.

I stretch time and sketch
arches, trees and bells,
opposite the Roman Forum,
sipping a heart-topped
cappuccino, ignoring the
persistent pleas of a beggar, who
points to his yapping dog
to accentuate my guilt.

The band's bridged into
"Oh When The Saints
Go Marching Home,"
and a silver statue of
Lady Liberty is
lifting her torch
near the traffic lights,
but nobody cares.

Every day
is the day after,
but some more
than others, and
I particularly like

this one that just
trundles along
at a walking pace.

I think back to the time
I first visited the soot
covered Coliseum
when you could
simply walk in –
and stray dogs roamed
the bowels of the ruins
keeping the homeless company.

I think forward
and get as far as the afternoon,
and that's good enough for me.
King Tut and Liberty
on either side of the street band
are still freezing for handouts,
while the saxophonist leans into
"Sentimental Journey."

The sun's shining
through fragrant wisteria,
hanging light from the pergola
and I'm at peace – almost.

~ April 25, Rome, Italy, sitting in a café sipping a
cappuccino

1913
(At the Alte Nationalgalerie, Berlin, Germany)

- - -V
1913

⌢·
Life die-versions

⌢ Café concerts
Can-can dancers
Some fleeting sex…
While heavy crows
Flap over snow ⌢

Dégagé flâneur
Of nighttime Paris
London and Berlin
Drowns the hiss of
A l'arme' across Europe ⌢·

Heat of the day
Bathing, boating
Eating, drinking
Into moonlit
Trysts at lampposts ⌢·

Oppressive undercurrents
Go undetected
As the diversion frenzy
Fuels the ritual death dance ⌢·

Sacré souci

††††††††††††††††

unbuttoned dress

unbuttoned her dress
dressed her button
her "buts" addressed
his hooded head

bus stop   waited
called   texted   no reply
visited   knocked   voices
no answer

she cried   he lied
dumped him
stumped him
moved on   more fun

she caught his I
he caught her O
both caught –
knot tied

Abandoned Couplets

Boomers and late bloomers
fight over who gets the tickets.

Nowhere is there more compost
than north of the Plum Street commercial.

Shingles burn through velvet screams
turning delight into ribbons of red.

Filtered rancor fuels mistakes
camouflaged with placebo paste.

Botox wrinkles of an oiled cougar
conjures mink smiles and money.

A hum rattles the loose screw
with sympathetic vibrations.

Inanimate gadgets unite
to squirm in discomfort.

No thread is linked
least of all the red.

Time to abandon these
random, inane couplets.

*Words in a Bottle

       rib-
  boned.   and
A   sealed
  rolled   paper
     piece of

A sleeping beauty lying on a soft pink pillow
~~~~O

His hands trembled as
he................r.e..a...c....h.....e......d
for this G L A S S S sss env-elope
knowing that some-'dinc' will be un-veiled

bUt! UnsUre if his **life** woUld
E_____V_____E_____R
be the same again
     same again
        again
     …. gain….
the cork came out ease-lilly
& the cats on the papyrus
sat & watched in the margins
&   &
&   &
&   &
&   &
He placed the bottle aside [□□]
un^tied the crimson band
and b'ro'ke the emerald seal

and un-r--o---l----l----e-----d the epistle

THREE BOLD WORDS
       ! !!!! !!!
stared at him and he
              fell
              to
              his
              knees

       and shouted
"!YesSheDoes! ! !SheDoes!"
       ! !!!! !!!

Waking up on the Beach

Squint the ears
against bright traffic
and see calm caves
swim the breaking air

Taste the night-howl's breath
above table-tapping smoke-talk
and steady the rising tug
of belly-fingered songs

Touch the waves' salt-wet smiles
as they lap the funeral shore
and earn the ocean's spread
receding into blue

~ *Patmos/Samos, Greece*

Two Haiku

The pain won't stop
But will shorten its span
when you decide to let go

*

I change my focus
useless news piles up as waste
I aim for the good

12 Tanka Written in Italy

on the marble floor
lured by Pantheon's blue sun
girl lies flat to gaze
through the age old cranium
to her future's guiding star

my empty mind grins
left to the senses' fine song
all twelve holding hands
swaying as one to the dance –
my opening petals filled

her left hand asks why
her palm is pure acceptance
her shroud in turmoil
while the right hand holds his death
and her calm face knows his life

~ Written after viewing Michelangelo's Pietà

the ripples of pain
trav'ling across time and space
into my heart's pulse
circulate as unspilled blood
in the form of words from all

daily we can make
new acquaintances and friends
in stores, cafes – streets
with few words or just one smile
even a glance can touch crowds

time to tinker some
threading apt words together
into a necklace
to give away or forget
or lose as sometimes happens

the woman in me
tells the man to listen up
he's hard of hearing –
ear in the shape of a heart
opens like a tolling bell

we did a sun dance
seven of us on a whim
to thwart wind and rain –
the trail above the ocean
cleared and we danced in our minds

life to the full
means to be emptied of all
then finding the zone –
heat of the sun dries the pool
a cloudburst fills it back up

there where birds sing
between statues, ponds and trees
a drone buzzes down
scattering songs to silence –
secrets flee into hedges

take space or make space
we do both but have a choice
the latter's like light
shining on the relation
between what makes or takes space

I'm hurt in my heart
I need to tell my story
will someone listen –
my beat and broken body
craves a heart to hear my hurt

Pantheon, Rome

Publication Credits

Many of the poems first appeared in the following publications: *Southern Cross Review; The Weekenders Magazine; Carnival Magazine; The Mind(less) Muse; Literbug; Our Day's Encounter; The Stone Hobo; Molt; Decades Review; The Write Place at the Write Time; Poetic Medicine; oldyellownotebook; Semolina Pilchard; Amaranthine Muses; The Rainbow Rose; Eunoia: Exercise Bowler; Yes, Poetry; Wizards of the Wind; Numinous: Spiritual Poet. "Allen Ginsberg in Atlantis" was first published in* Coffee on the Piano for You *(Adonis Press, 2008) in a slightly different version.*

About the Author

Eric G. Müller was born in Durban, South Africa. After graduating from the University of the Witwatersrand, Johannesburg, he continued his studies in England and Germany, focusing on drama, music and education. Together with his family he moved to Eugene, Oregon, where he taught for eight years. Since then he has lived in upstate New York, teaching music, drama, and English literature, at the Hawthorne Valley High School. He is also the director of Teacher Education at the Alkion Center.

www.ericgmuller.com

www.ingramcontent.com/pod-product-compliance
Lightning Source LLC
Chambersburg PA
CBHW062003040426
42447CB00010B/1894